Praise for

My Hero

The children of America's military servicemen and women experience life in a way that most of us never have. Frequent moves, separation from the parent(s) in service, and uncertainty about the next reunion become accepted facts of life. We are humbled by the dedication of the thousands of such families in Iraq, Afghanistan, and around the world.

My Hero paints an intimate portrait of the personal thoughts and emotions felt by these children. It clearly demonstrates, without reservation, the immense pride, honor, and unselfishness of our nation's military children and their families.

Jimmy Carter

39TH PRESIDENT OF THE UNITED STATES OF AMERICA

This book illustrates a wonderfully accurate picture of what the children of our military personnel go through when a parent is deployed. Their essays are simple and honest expressions of grief and sadness mixed with a tremendous sense of family pride and unparalleled patriotism.

The children of our military personnel are truly amazing. They are resilient when faced with frequent re-location; they handle life's difficulties with unfailing optimism (as exemplified in these essays); and they demonstrate courage when a parent is deployed in service to our country.

This book is a wonderful way to honor these children, many of whom will likely one day wear the uniform of our Armed Forces', and their parents'. They make us all proud to be Americans!

George H. W. Bush

41st PRESIDENT OF THE UNITED STATES OF AMERICA

Our men and women in uniform bravely defend our nation, and we owe them a profound debt of gratitude. Too often, though, we overlook the sacrifices made by their families. The members of America's military answer the call of duty and defend our freedom every day. When they are deployed around the world, precious family time is lost. But in spite of the great distances that often separate them, our troops are heroic role models to their kids. No one could better express our nation's gratitude to them than their courageous, resilient, and loving children.

With this heartwarming collection of essays and artwork, the many mothers and fathers in the United States military can take comfort knowing how much their service means to their families. Each work in this volume was created with one beloved family member in mind, but taken together, they form a touching tribute to all of those parents, past and present, who have served our country so faithfully.

William Jefferson Clinton

42nd PRESIDENT OF THE UNITED STATES OF AMERICA

Emma Mallets, age 11

My Hero

EDITED BY

Allen Appel and Mike Rothmiller

FOREWORD BY

General H. Norman Schwarzkopf

ST. MARTIN'S PRESS ≋ NEW YORK

My Hero

Military Kids

Write About Their

Moms and Dads

www.stmartins.com

ISBN-13: 978-0-312-37346-7
ISBN-10: 0-312-37346-5

First Edition: May 2008

10 9 8 7 6 5 4 3 2 1

Acknowledgments

It is a great honor for us to thank General H. Norman Schwarzkopf for his foreword and the kind words of endorsement from Presidents Jimmy Carter, George Herbert Walker Bush, and William Jefferson Clinton.

We would like to thank the Armed Services YMCA for all the fine work they do to enhance the lives of servicemen and women and their children. In particular, we thank National Executive Director RADM S. Frank Gallo, USN (Ret.), Deputy National Director CAPT Mike Landers, USN (Ret.), Susan Simms, Col George Brown, USMC (Ret.) and Col Lee Farmer, USMC (Ret.), all of whom were patient and thorough in answering our questions and supplying us with the original material. Anyone wishing to find out more about this great organization and how they could contribute to the work being done is urged to go to www.asymca.org.

And then there's the kids. Always the kids. The hundreds and hundreds who wrote essays and drew pictures and made us understand how proud they are of their moms and dads, the military, and their country. And made all of us understand how proud we are of them.

—Allen Appel and Mike Rothmiller

Foreword

American servicemen and women are the greatest soldiers in the world. As individuals and as a group, they are smart, tough, tenacious, and possess unlimited amounts of courage. Their patriotism knows no bounds. I believe these same characteristics also make them the finest parents in the world. They have a strong moral sense that is so important in raising children and equipping them for life in our challenging times.

In these pages kids from military families were asked to name their heroes. Here are their answers. They are funny, sad, perceptive, and, above all, honest. Sometimes heartbreakingly so. With parents like these, with children like these, our country's future will never be in doubt.

—General H. Norman Schwarzkopf

Charles Kim, age 11

He is in Iraq. As bullets fly by him and bombs explode, my dad still writes to my family, telling us to keep our chins high. My mom has had her third baby, his name is Breydon he is only 2 weeks old, I love him so much and my dad longs to see him! My sister's name is Brittany we get in lots of fights but my dad says to make sure I try not to get in anymore fights with her so he doesn't worry. My mom and grandma are worried about my dad and they help me not to cry while my dad is away. Time will go fast and I look forward to dad coming home when he will swing me in his strong arms and say, "Let's go fishing son."

—Brandon Jordan Hansen, age 8

AIR FORCE: MSGT LEO C. HANSEN

My mom is Sergeant Fore. She is a drill instructor in the Marine Corps, so I don't get to see her that much. If your mom or dad is in the Marine Corps you know how that feels.

—Ladasia Logan, age 7

MARINES: SGT KENYADA FORE

My dad is an HMCS (Senior Chief Hospital Corpsman). Basically everyone calls him Senior Chief Willis. He is currently an E8. (I, personally, am looking forward to a promotion to E9 so my family can obtain good parking.) He is ready to serve, anywhere, anytime. Although he does not fly around in a cape or wear his underwear outside his pants, he does save a world—my world.

—Jazzmine Willis, age 12

NAVY: SCPO RENEE WILLIS

Veronica Mcleod, age 8

Two years ago a very unfortunate thing happened to him. He was diagnosed with cancer; even though he had just gotten surgery and wasn't very strong he still requested to be stationed in Kuwait and his request was granted. He is now a three-year survivor of cancer. My dad also has a really good sense of humor. Even when he tries to be funny but isn't we find something to laugh about anyway. No matter what he does he tries and he NEVER gives up. I am 13 years old and I still think my dad is the coolest, strongest, and best dad in the world. We may fight a lot, but he will always be my hero.

—Sarah Pearson, age 13

ARMY: SFC ROBERT J. PEARSON

My dad is my hero because he was my dad. He
took care of us before himself. He always played with
all of us and he helped me in sports. He was busy in the
Army but always made time to spend with our family. We
shared a love and interest in collecting baseball cards.
My dad taught me to respect people and encouraged me
to do my best. My dad was also my hero because he was
in the Army. He protected our country in Afghanistan.
His men built a school for the children there and Dexter
students sent books for them. My dad was killed in
action in Afghanistan on October 31, 2006 by an IED. Now
he is a war hero.

—Aidan Sloan, age 11

ARMY: MAJ DOUGLAS SLOAN (KIA)

Christopher Lipscomb, age 10

He is an American soldier. He has gone to faraway places. He has left family and friends to do his duty. I miss my daddy a lot, and I want him to come back, but I understand why he is in Afghanistan. He will always remember me every day. He sends me pictures on the computer. He is sacrificing his life for me and world freedom. He has faith and hope and he will give it to the world. And he has said I am the beat of his heart. He is the beat of my heart too! I miss him so very much.

—Ariel Wilson, age 7

ARMY: SFC RAMAH WILSON

My dad is my hero because he tucks me into bed and sometimes helps me with my homework and he loves me very much. My dad is also other people's hero because he flew over to places that had wars and gave the people fighting lots of food and things. He always lends a hand to everyone who needs it.

—Kathryn Bistodeau, age 8

AIR FORCE: LTCOL BRADLEY BISTODEAU

He has served in the military for over 21 years. The only reason we can lie down at night, shut our eyes and dream our dreams is because of people like my father.

—Samantha A. Beyers, age 13

ARMY: MAJ BRUCE BEYERS

Kirstyn Wesala, age 11

When a hero comes to mind you usually think of a man dressed in bright colors rather than a woman in A.C.Us. She not only fights for me but the whole country. She has been shipped to Korea, the desert, and Afghanistan, and I'm proud of my mother because she is stronger, braver, and tougher from being in the army. I don't know if she will go to Iraq but I know that she is strong, so I think she will be OK.

—Thomas Overtree, age 13

ARMY: SSG MELINDA SESSOMS

My dad is a life saver and a heart breaker. He is mighty. My daddy is a fighter. He is always in my heart. My dad goes to Iraq and stands up to the battle. He is my best dad of the world.

—Brandon Shelton, age 8

ARMY: SSG JOSEPH A. SHELTON

Boom! The tank bombed the house with some of the Iraqi soldiers in it. My dad and two of his friends went into the building; my dad went to the right door, Lt. Jenkins went through the left door, Major Doyle went into the center door. All together they killed ten and captured five Iraqi soldiers. My dad protects the country from Danger and he will risk his life for the country just like all the other parents in the military. He loves animals, especially our dog Lucky.

—Colin Ryan, age 12

ARMY: MAJ ROBERT RYAN

As heart breaking as it is to know my father is in the U.S. Army, going to Iraq constantly, I am proud to say my father is my military hero. I say this because I know my father doesn't only do this because he wants to serve his country, but because this is his passion, what he wanted to do. My father is a loving father and husband as well as a strong soldier. He knows how to have lots of fun and still be a great soldier. I was proud of my father when he got an award for saving another soldier's life from a truck that was about to explode. I was really proud. I don't have the power to know what happens to my father when he leaves but when he comes back home I'll give him a big hug and then I'll know that he is safe.

—Sharim E. Torres, age 13

ARMY: SPC LUIS E. ARROYO

My dad is an awesome role model to me. One time the lady at the PX gave my dad too much change, so he went back and gave her the extra back.

—Hadley Boberg, age 13

ARMY: MAJ WILLIAM BOBERG

My mom was a very great Airman. She died doing her job. She loved wearing her uniform. I loved seeing her in it. She never missed work because she was never sick. She made us do our homework. She always helped her friends. She never let her friends down. She was a great person.

—Zachari Perri, age 6

AIR FORCE: SRA ABBY BILBREY (DECEASED)

My dad is my hero because he teaches me to be confident and sets the example to take pride in my work by doing it himself. Even though it scares me when he goes to war, I know he's coming back having accomplished something good. This thing is giving freedom to our country and to others too. One day I am going to be just like him. I will be noble, understanding, kind, and inspiring, just like my father. Even though I am grounded most of the time, he usually goes easy on me. When my father is at his deathbed I will avenge him and take up where he left off. Then I shall be as successful as he is. I know my father believes in God so I know he will go to heaven and be in a better place. I will be happy for him but sad because he is not here telling me how to do things. I love my father and he loves me.

—Mark Estrada, age 10

ARMY: MAJ MARCOS ESTRADA

She's nice to everyone. She lets me have a sleepover.
She lets me go to the carnival. She helps me with my
homework. She helps my friends when they fall off
their bikes.

—Hunter Burbank, age 7

AIR FORCE: TSGT DENISE ZIWISKY

She doesn't care what anyone says about me, she still
loves me. She was brave enough to go to Kuwait. My
mom is such a hero to me, even in my heart.

—Kelsey Hover, age 11

NATIONAL GUARD: SPC CARY TRABAL

He puts happiness in my life, when mom is not here he lets me cuddle with him, he helped me win a game of dominoes, at Christmas he gives me the best things, he makes me my favorite food when I want it, he sometimes lets me play on his computers, he fixes my computer when it is broken, he helps me clean my room, he puts my favorite movies on for me to watch, he helps save American soldiers from dying in the war, and he works to buy really good things to make our family very strong.

—Veronica King, age 6

ARMY: LTC RONALD KING

He is fighting for our country. I don't know where he is right now. But I do know he is helping hurt soldiers because he is a dermatologist wherever he is. I am proud of him. And even if he wasn't in war he would still be doing what he does like taking care of skin and stuff. If it wasn't for people like my dad who knows how to make skin better and lots of other cool things, then we would not be able to care for hurt skin on people because no one would be able to work the laser for taking tattoos off. So they would have tattoos for life and that would stink.

—William Peters, age 11

ARMY: LTC JOHN PETERS

Jacob Snow, age 12

The important thing about a hero is they make us safe. They are drug free and are very nice. They don't brag. They just do what they are supposed to do. That is hard work. My daddy is my hero. He gets up early. Daddy goes to P.T. Then he comes home and takes a shower. Ready for work again. Daddy used to work at Little Caesars as a second job. Now daddy is in Afghanistan. I got three e-mails from him and a card from him too. It has a happy face. It was cute and sweet. It made me cry because I miss him so, and he will miss my birthday. He always makes it special. He is very nice. Daddy always does his best. Daddy has very hard work. Daddy works in tanks! He fights in wars to keep up the flag. Just for America.

—Taylor Paul, age 8

ARMY: SSG JOHN PAUL

My mom is my hero because she cooks for me so that I don't starve. She's nice to me and my friends too. She saves me because she is in the Air Force.

—Hannah Dunks, age 7

AIR FORCE: TSGT JENNIFER DUNKS

My mom fights for freedom. She is training in Texas. She'll catch bad guys in Iraq. My dad fixes the flight simulator. My grandpa is in the Air Force. He is a pilot. He won a battle.

—Matthew Klempp, age 9

AIR FORCE: MAJ TONYA KLEMPP AND LT MATT KLEMPP

If my mom ever were to die I would forever cry. My mom works in the Navy and has my whole life. As my mom works and works she put her life on the line for yours, mine, and our country. We are lucky to have people like my mom on the planet. She is one of the thousands of people who are confident, loyal, forgiving, and trust-worthy with all of their hearts. I salute my mom; there couldn't be anything better in the whole wide world.

—John Harvey, age 11

NAVY: HM2 RACHELLE HARVEY

My dad is my hero because he went to Iraq when I was turning four. He helped strangers and people he didn't know. I think he is the strongest man in the world.

—Ally Heitink, age 7

MARINE CORPS: SSGT JAY D. HEITINK

My dad is my hero because he makes me laugh when I am scared. He protects me everyday and night. Sometimes I think he can fly like Superman. I'll always be his little girl. I am his only little girl and he is my only dad. Even if he yells at me, he is still my dad and I will still love him a lot.

—Abagail Frantzen, age 7

NAVY: CPO KENNETH FRANTZEN

My mom is a foot doctor in the U.S. Army. She helps people by looking at a person's foot. She sometimes has to work through lunchtime. She always helps me with my feet, too. Every day my mom sees about 20 patients or more. She takes care of me and plays games with me. She keeps us all moving in the right direction.

—Robert Osborn, age 8

ARMY: LTC JACKIE CHEN

She used to be a Sergeant in the Marine Corps. Being in the Marines has made an impact in her life. This impact has changed her from being a troubled youth into a woman with self-discipline, integrity, and honor. She lives by those values on a daily basis and shows her children why those values are so important. Even though she is no longer in the Marines she is still a hero for me. She always used to tell me "You can take the girl out of the Marines, but you can't take the Marine out of the girl."

—Kylie Dillinger, age 13

MARINES: SGT LORI POPP

My dad is my hero because he jumps out of planes and gets the bad guys to make the world safe. I would be so scared to jump from a plane. He keeps our country safe too. I love my dad because he is working hard to take care of me. He makes maps for the Army, lots of maps! The maps help his boss find where the bad guys are camping at. They are not treasure maps, they are bad guy maps. When he is not in Afghanistan, he comes home to play with me every night. I don't like that my dad had to leave but I know that he is keeping the planet safe. My dad is the best dad in the world and he is a good food cook. Someday I want to be big and strong like my dad and drive a jeep. I wish he had an easy job and not a hard job. When he is gone, he puts me in charge of our house and it is a hard job to do.

—John Ward Tatum III, age 6

ARMY: WO1 JOHN TATUM JR.

I am proud of my military dad because he fights for freedom and not for war. He is like a thick plate of armor protecting us. He is like a very bright night. My dad goes on long deployments. I don't like that because I miss him. When he went away he helped Iraq and other countries. I am proud of my dad because he seems like the bravest person ever to live.

—Sean Callahan, age 7

MARINES: LTCOL TIMOTHY CALLAHAN

The important thing about heroes is that they come from all over the world. They can be fat or skinny. They can be old or young. They can be from any state or any country. They can be small or tall. Another thing about

Gabrielle Tan, age 10

heroes is that they think about others. My dad is an American soldier from Utah. He is my hero. He cooked for me every night when he was home. Then we found out some horrible news. He had to go to war for $2\frac{1}{2}$ years. And now it's just me, my two sisters, my stepmom and my little brother. Now I get to see him on the computer. On the computer he says "Hey" and I say hey is for horses and he laughs. My mother talks to him about serious stuff. I don't think this war will end in 2007. This is his third time going to Iraq. My dad never gives up. When he comes back I will give him a big hug. He will always be my hero and be in my heart.

—Tessa Wilcox, age 8

ARMY: SSG RYAN S. WILCOX

27

My dad is a warrant officer in the Marine Corps. He takes care of my family. He fixes things for me. He takes me places. My mom takes me to fast foods and my dad does not like fast foods. He likes Superman. He loves me. He loves my mom. He loves Georgia and Flash, those are my dogs. My dad is gone. We have two more months until he comes back. I miss him all the way to Mars from Earth.

—Blaise Giove, age 7

MARINES: SGT STEPHEN GIOVE

My dad can do 45 sit-ups in one minute and thirty one push-ups in one minute. He can run 2 miles in 5 minutes!

—Destanie Heslar, age 9

ARMY: PFC KERR CHRISTOPHER

My dad is my hero not because he is my dad but for his bravery and courage that he puts on the line every day. He risks his life for his family, friends and so we can have our freedom. If I could make a memorial statue of him it will be 900 feet high. It will be fantastic. It will have his name, ADRIAN on it. The statue will be amazing. It will be made to honor him.

—Esperanza Rosales, age 9

ARMY: SSG ADRIAN ROSALES

There are four elements to my dad's heroics. First, we have stunning times when he is at home. It is like a marvelous run of fun. When we wrestle he is a menacing ball of terrifying termites. He seems to have a good skill at picking movies too. When we camp it is always an adventure with dad. We have delectable marshmallows and junk food all day. Next, he is my hero when he is in Iraq (besides when he leaves). We see pictures that have places that he has been. The statues are so delightful with artistic details. He brings home Dutch chocolates. His messages are like a writing of heroic mysteries. They make me feel good. Third, my dad is my hero because he always helps me. For example, he helps with my homework. I always get stuck on that. Or the time he untied a very strong knot on a tree. Finally, my hero and I have a lot in common. I think we both wake up early (that's for sure!). We love to get athletic. He seems smart like he passed 3,000,000 years of college. I think I'm smart too. We are similar.

—Shepard Todd Petit, age 8

ARMY: LTC BRIAN SHEPARD PETIT

Whenever I get very sick I have my mom to help me. Not that my dad isn't also my hero, but I usually see more of my mom than my dad because he works more. Even though I don't like it much, she limits what I can watch on TV. Another thing about my mom is she comforts my brother, sister and me when we are sad. She cooks most of our meals and once a week we go out to eat.

—Robert Anthony Windom Jr., age 12

NAVY: LT ROBERT WINDOM AND CHARLOTTE WINDOM

She cooks food every day. She helped me when I fell off my bike. Mom picked me up and carried me home. She wiped my sores and the blood and she put me in the tub. I felt happy. My mom knows how to hotwire a car. We were traveling to Alabama then we crashed and a wire fell out of place. She got out my dad's tools and she hotwired it and made it to Alabama. I felt good. I love my mom and have a good time with her! Her name is Tetra.

—Butler Nicklus, age 7

MARINES: SSGT ANTONIO MCKENZIE

He can run 5 miles in 15 minutes. He can do 100 pushups in a minute. He also saves me from anything that will hurt me. He jumps from planes at the drop zone. He can fix lots of things like the car, the sink, my bike, and the dishwasher. He is a sweet and kind man.

—Megan Thomas, age 9

ARMY: CPT JOSEPH LARRY THOMAS

My stepdad, Michael Gardner, is my hero because he has to go to war, jumps out of airplanes, went to Fort Gordon, Georgia, for school, and took all of his family out to dinner at Golden Corral.

—Cheyenne Slaton, age 10

ARMY: SSG MICHAEL GARDNER

Nathaniel Tripp, age 11

My dad is a military police. He helps people follow the law who are not following the law. My dad throws these people in jail. Mom takes care of us. She takes care of our two dogs, Hades and Jackie. My mom takes care of my family every day, rain or shine.

—Aspen Abram, age 10

ARMY: SSG DAVID BURKS AND JENNIFER BURKS

An important aspect my mom has is she can "put up with me." She doesn't yell at me just because I'm not on task. The only time she yells at me is when I'm in trouble. She makes me finish my homework every night. She snaps me back to reality when I doze off.

—Kaleb Dunks, age 11

AIR FORCE: TSGT JENNA DUNKS

My dad is the best soldier because he works on computers and installs software. He taught me how to cook gumbo. We make great gumbo. My dad is my hero, he saved me from a fire. He took my mom out for their anniversary. My dad can run 75 laps around the track.

—Jerrel Elder, age 9

ARMY: SGT JERREL ELDER SR.

My Dad is a Master Sergeant. My mom is a Captain. I love my mom's cooking but my dad's isn't that good. I love my parents very much and they are my military heroes.

—Jourdan Barrows, age 11

AIR FORCE: CAPT ANGELA BARROWS

AND MSGT STEVEN BARROWS

My dad is the First Sergeant of Bravo Company, "The Bulldogs." My dad trains hard because training is his number-one priority. My dad takes care of his soldiers and makes them do a lot of push-ups to help them remember to wear the proper uniform. My dad does push-ups all the time and can do 75 in two minutes. He runs a lot and even loves to play football and soccer, although he is 44 years old. My dad does not like to watch sports on television any more, which is good for my brother and I to watch our shows. Even though my dad is very busy, never misses a meeting, and comes home late every day, he still finds time to help me with my homework. He always tells the best bedtime stories. My favorites are about the adventures of "Mike" and

"Nella," two children whose names are mine and my brother Allen's spelled backwards. My dad also tells stories about a boy from a long time ago. He doesn't say what the boy's name is, but I know that the boy's name is Bruce (my dad). He never forgets to pray for and with me as well. He has taught me many values which have helped me to be a good person. My dad went to Iraq twice. He sent me many e-mails and called quite often. My dad likes the Army because he gets paid to do many fun things like shoot weapons, exercise, go inside a gas chamber, walk many miles with a rucksack, and jump out of airplanes. My dad doesn't know what he wants to do when he grows up. No matter what, I love my dad, even when he raises his voice when I'm not being good. My dad is my hero.

—Kimberly Kavinsky, age 9

ARMY: 1SG BRUCE KAVINSKY

She went to fight the war on terrorism in Iraq. When she was in Iraq she tested the water to ensure it was safe to drink for everyone who lived on the base. She was just accepted to an officer program to become an Air Force nurse. She wants to become a nurse so she can take care of all the wounded soldiers coming home from the war.

—Johnathon Greenhoe, age 9

AIR FORCE: TSGT JENIFER GREENHOE

She works hard for our country to be safe. My mom helps poor people by giving them the stuff I don't need any more. She is a master sergeant in the Air Force. My mom could be a famous person one day.

—Astrid Sletten, age 7

AIR FORCE: MSGT CASSANDRA SLETTEN

When my father went over to Iraq, he did something that always makes me smile. He passed candy out to all the little kids who were stranded on the streets of Iraq. Think of how long it had been since they had eaten something so sweet. Think of how long it had been for them to know that someone actually cared. My dad is like a puzzle piece to me. Without him, nothing works properly; nothing fits like it should. He makes me feel safe and admits when he is wrong. To me, a dad like this doesn't come around like rain in the forest does. I can always trust him no matter what happens. My dad doesn't swing from webs or wrestle Joker. My dad doesn't have those abilities. But he does have what it takes to be my hero.

—Ellie Varicak, age 11

MARINES: MAJ MICHAEL VARICAK

41

My dad has deployed six times to support the war. He
is one of America's bravest; he's a firefighter. He runs in
to danger while everyone runs away. He is now deployed
to Baghdad, a very dangerous place. While my dad
is in Baghdad he still finds time to write to me; he also
gives the clothes and shoes I can't fit to the Iraqi kids.
He's willing to make sacrifices like no one else I know.
When he calls home he never complains. He also found
time to call me on my birthday. This is to my dad,
my unsung hero. He may never have his name in lights,
and people may never know the sacrifices he makes
for me and my family and our country. But I will always
celebrate him.

—Mercedes Gillon-Gantt, age 12

AIR FORCE: SSGT KEVIN GANTT

Right now my dad is not here, he is in Iraq. Hopefully he gets back safe. If he didn't I will know what happened, he turned in his gun and his uniform and everything else for those beloved, holy, beautiful white wings of heaven. Like my dad said, "Once a Marine, always a Marine."

—Raymond Joseph Shew, age 13

MARINES: GYSGT SHAWN M. DEMPSEY

She takes care of people and makes sure our whole country is safe and strong. When people see my mom they always smile because they know she is a blessed and smart woman.

—Psalms Doucettperry, age 7

ARMY: MAJ MARIA DOUCETTPERRY

Mom was in the army and fell out of a truck and hurt her back. She has MS which means Multiple Sclerosis so she has to take shots every other day. I still love her even though she grounds me a lot and yells at me. She helps me from when I am sad from other people making fun of me cause I am small. She says that I am sweet, caring and a good friend when I stood up for my best friend, Shara.

—Kanyon Wilson, age 11

ARMY: SPC REGINA DIANE DUCH

Then came the day when he had to deploy to Afghanistan, the day I burst into tears and wouldn't stop. But I knew he would be back, standing there waiting for me to jump into his arms and never let me go. A few days later I started to receive e-mails and letters from him. When he came back I couldn't let him go, I just couldn't see him leave again. He explained to me that being in the military, he needs to protect and defend our country. I now know why he's in the Air Force, he loves to help other people, he protects our country like he protects me and he believes that everyone can make a difference. Someday I will grow up and be just like him, honest, caring, and thoughtful. And along the way I know he will be standing right next to me to guide me there.

—Emily Elisabeth Rhea, age 11

AIR FORCE: TSGT CHARLES D. RHEA

My dad is my hero because instead of being a bum he gets up in the morning to go to work and I've never heard him complain about going to work. I think if he had the day off, instead of sleeping the whole day he would get up and cook breakfast for my brother, sister and me. He would do the laundry, wash the dishes, and he would pick us up after school like a mom would do. Most dads would have their wives do these things but not my dad; he's like a mister mom! Even though I miss him while he's on a TDY I understand that it is his job to keep a bunch of families safe. Sometimes he may feel like he doesn't get thanks for everything he does but he will always get thanks from me. Most important, if he ever quit or lost his job he would always be my hero because he has taught me a big lesson. If you do things for your family, you will get something in return: A good life!

—Alicia Reynolds, age 11

AIR FORCE: MSGT BRIAN REYNOLDS

I think he fought in a war. He is a drill sergeant. He
shoots guns down range. He is special. He is my hero!
He works hard. My dad teaches soldiers. My dad is nice
and mean to the soldiers at the same time. My dad
teaches soldiers how to crawl. My dad teaches soldiers in
the woods. My dad knows how to treat the soldiers.
My dad is tired, hungry and smells when he gets home
sometimes. My dad does a lot of things in the Army. My
dad works his heart off!

—Joseph R. Diaz, age 8

ARMY: SFC RUBEN DIAZ

My dad, Marcus, is strong because he can pick up a 50-pound weight. He can pick it up with one hand. He is also strong because he can do 100 sit-ups without one glass of water. My dad does a lot of P.T. in the Army. I love him. He is the greatest.

—Analysa Cassanova-Smith, age 8

ARMY: SFC MARCUS F. SMITH

Being in the military may be hard, but that all pays off when you know you are helping your country. She's kind, but doesn't give in, which builds a sturdy family. It's not the medals or even the uniform, it's how much you care and sacrifice. I know there are more parents out there who are unknown heroes; I hope to be one too.

—Jessie Reeves, age 10

NAVY: CAPT NANCY REEVES

Shae Corey, age 8

In a land far away an Army soldier was captured and held hostage. My dad participated in her rescue. It was a cold night and he was scared. He was in danger of being shot at by the enemy. He went on and the rescue succeeded. Hero—a courageous, brave, noble person who does a deed despite getting in harm's way. My dad demonstrated that he was a hero by going in harm's way to do a good deed, flying in Special Forces troops to rescue Pfc. Jessica Lynch.

—Cody Anderson-Parks, age 9

MARINES: LTCOL JAMES ANDERSON II

Psalms Doucettperry, age 7

My dad is in the military and he is a Gunny. He bosses people around. He is so bored in his office because it is so hot in there and there is nothing to do.

—Devin Ward, age 10

MARINES: GYSGT BUFF WARD

My mom comes home late at night from her job at Ft. Bragg. No matter how tired she is she always takes time to say good night. She can run 2 miles in 16 minutes and do 50 pull-ups in 3 minutes. Sometimes my mother can be so silly. My mom's first language is Spanish. I speak Spanish too. Mi mami es la major mami del mundo. That means my mom is the best mom in the world.

—Jennifer Patino, age 9

ARMY: PFC CLAUDIA STALLINGS

He is energetic, funny, joyful and kind. Dad puts his life on the line every day, and he is loyal to his mission. My father is currently deployed to Iraq. We get letters and e-mails from him, and we love them when we aren't so happy. My mom sometimes feels under the weather. When my hero comes home things will be a lot different.

—Zechariah Snel, age 10

ARMY: MAJ JOSEPH A. SNEL

My mom is a great role model because she volunteers a lot and never gets in trouble with her boss. She's very generous when she donates to charity and is not greedy when she tips people unless they do a bad job. She is a very loving mother.

—Cotey Pierce, age 12

NAVY: PO3 TINA PIERCE

He is super nice, helpful and brave. Whenever I feel down he cheers me up. He is very selfless. Plus, he relieves all my stress. In addition, my father is willing to talk to me about anything that sets my teeth on edge. My dad is also very protective. He would guard me tooth and nail if necessary. Right now my dad is deployed to Iraq. He is gone for many months, and we don't know exactly when he will come back, but he will return soon. I can't wait until that day.

—Jake McCrea, age 11

ARMY: LTC MICHAEL V. MCCREA

He is a fire chief. My dad tells fire fighters where the fire is. He also tells them where to go so they don't get trapped. If they don't get trapped families still have their mothers and fathers. Even though he has a big important job, he can provide for us. He provides food like meat, drinks, fruit, vegetables and my favorite, French Fries! I also remember when he was a fire fighter he saved a little baby. He also got a father out of a burning, falling building. I can't believe he jumped into a burning building! Jim, my dad, is a real hero.

—Samuel Niall Lindsey age 12

AIR FORCE: MSGT JAMES E. LINDSEY

Clink, clink, clink. Boom! The sounds of bullets hitting metal. A missile. These are the sounds my dad hears almost every day. He's been in Iraq for six months now. In that time he's had Marines fall down before him. He's been shot at and a helicopter crashed with him in it! In that crash he survived, our friend's dad didn't. I had never had someone that close to me die in war before. I see now that my Dad will die to protect me, to protect other people everywhere and to protect America. In Iraq my dad has found road bombs and criminals everywhere. Now he is helping tell some tribe leaders to get volunteers for the Iraqi police. The more the Iraqis can handle the less the marines are needed. I found an article on the Internet that says a couple of quotes like, "I won't leave until I hear there's enough Iraqi police." That's my same old Dad! Everything is thorough with him.

—Kate Donnellan, age 11

MARINES: LTCOL JAMES E. DONNELLAN

Dasia Lang, age 9

He fights for freedom. He respects how other people are, their religion and their skin color. He is against slavery. Papa is my hero because he always holds to me. Papa is my hero, just my hero because I love him for the things he does. The good things he does to others and to me. If he wasn't here I wouldn't have someone to wipe my tears off my cheek. Papa gives the poor people on the street money. I love my Papa.

—Shaniquah Lipki, age 11

ARMY: SSG CHRISTOPHER L. BELT

He fixes helicopters and airplanes so that the Army people can get to where they have to go and because he makes sure the airplanes don't crash when they are in the air. He gave up smoking to work harder because he didn't have to take so much time to go on smoke breaks.

—Sean Brannon, age 12

AIR FORCE: MSGT JOHN J. BRANNON

During my dad's deployment he was involved in a mission where he helped save the lives of many other soldiers. He is an Apache Longbow Pilot. Because of this act, my dad received the Distinguished Flying Cross award just a few months ago. It was very exciting to watch my dad receive this award but at the same time it was very scary. A soldier read a paper of what my dad had done to earn this award and he kept saying that my dad flew into the path of the enemy. How scary is that? He did not do it just once; he did it a bunch of times. I thought to myself he had to have been crazy! But then I realized something, my dad was so brave. He put so many others before himself. Just knowing that he would risk his life for the lives of others was something to really take in and be proud of.

—Brittany Learn, age 12

ARMY: CW2 PHILIP LEARN

She's like my guardian angel. When I'm hurt she's my doctor. When I feel like I can't do something mom encourages me and tells me I can do it. When I get something wrong, she doesn't get mad, she just says try again. My mom is always happy. When I make a mess she doesn't yell she just says "Nyesha, clean your mess up, please."

—Nyesha Brownlee, age 9

NATIONAL GUARD: SGT RENEE BROWNLEE

My dad enjoys being a U.S. marine and only has $2\frac{1}{2}$ more years until he is going to be a major. He is still pretty far from General. Like 20 years and if my dad continues I will be 30 by the time my dad has completed all ranks.

—Cathryn Thompson, age 10

MARINES: CAPT HARRY THOMPSON

Jasmin Conyers, age 14

My dad is my hero because he raids houses and controls a whole platoon. He is a captain. He rides in Strykers all the time. He has been in Iraq for almost 2 years. Sometimes they use flash grenades because they could be ambushed. He is 30 years old and he raided buildings most of the time he was in Iraq. After that he went to Baghdad.

—Roland Lester, age 10

ARMY: CPT ROLAND LESTER

To begin with, my dad is very nice looking. He has black hair, brown eyes, Hispanic skin and loves baseball and golf. (Just like me!) He always has his shirt tucked in and always looks his best. His very important qualities that I love about him are that he is very nice, friendly, and always acts like he is 20. My dad trains sailors so they can help protect the United States. After teaching he goes out and works on a big ship. He can steer the ship in an easy and steady way. My dad travels a lot at the last minute. He goes to the mainland more times than you can think of: San Diego, Jacksonville, and even Virginia. He went to the war in Iraq. I really missed him!

—Courtney Ortega, age 10

NAVY: SCPO PATRICK B. ORTEGA

My dad works in the Air Force. He has been serving for 23 years. That is a LONG time to serve your country. He flies E-3s. It is a plane that has BIG radar on top that is used for finding enemy airplanes. So, if there are any wars by where my dad is, he will go in the E-3 and find those enemy airplanes. Those enemy airplanes will wish that they had never been built!

—Meghan Duffey, age 10

AIR FORCE: CMSGT RUSSELL DUFFEY

She works hard as a pathologist in the Navy. An important aspect is her personality. Prioritized, friendly, open, and caring, she makes friends quickly in a new hospital. Also, she tolerates mistakes and permits venting. She studies hard and can examine sick flesh without wincing. The responsibility is astounding. I love her beyond measure.

—Avery Nelson, age 12

NAVY: YN1 TIFFANY NELSON

Zachery Tyra, age 11

My dad hangs out with me and takes me everywhere I want to go. He takes me to my practices and never misses a game. Ever since I can remember he has always been there for me. When I am in trouble with my mom he is always there to defend me well. Sometimes it is the other way around. Sometimes I wonder why I have such a great dad. Why God put him in my life. I wonder what the world would be like without dads. The world would probably be very dull.

—Susi Wills, age 11

ARMY: CPT MATHEW L. GOLSTEYN

When I had a Christmas play there was this baby that had a seizure right in the middle of the play. So my mom ran out of the Christmas play and saved the baby. Everything was dead silent. Then when she came back she said the baby was ok. The mom of the baby was really grateful.

—Reed Hurdertmark, age 11

ARMY: CPT JULIE HURDERTMARK

68

One important reason my dad is my hero is because he cooks. He is always very busy with meetings, blabbing and making speeches and getting to know the people in the office. Anyways he does find time to cook, but not like eggs or bacon or anything like that. Speaking of eggs and bacon, one time I woke up and found everything in the kitchen black and smoky. It smelled like burnt rubber. The fire alarm was ringing and buzzing in my ears! The firemen came and, embarrassed, my dad explained he had tried to make bacon and eggs for breakfast. That was hilarious! He always makes me laugh too. From that day on my dad sticks to grilling and barbequing and as far away from the stove as possible.

—Katie Deal, age 11

AIR FORCE: MAJ MIKE DEAL

Without him I would not know what do because he loves me so very much. I always want to do a good job so he will be proud of me. He is always telling jokes or fooling around doing anything he can to get a laugh out of me and my brother. We always have a great time together. My daddy will soon deploy and I wish him all the luck while he is gone. I will pray every night that he will be home soon. All I want is him home safely again. I love him with all my heart. He is not just my daddy but my best friend too.

—Laura Isabel Gilchrist, age 11

NAVY: CPO CRAIG L. GILCHRIST

My dad has been to Iraq and Afghanistan. He says it is not that cool. He was a Navy SEAL. He traveled to Malaysia and he ate monkey brains there! I was 3 when he was in the Navy. He used to get me out of bed to see the fireworks when we lived in Coronado, California. My dad is an Army Ranger. I think he is very brave.

Emilly Mueller, age 10

ARMY: CPT STEVEN MUELLER

My mom is a big hero because she plays football. She rides bikes with us. She watches movies with us. She takes me everywhere. When I am sick she goes out in the cold to buy me medicine. She throws me birthday parties. She puts food on the table. She gives me money to go bowling every Friday. She takes me to the hospital when I broke my chin. She is the most loveable mom ever.

—Markeith Perry, age 12

MARINES: 1STSGT EUGENE LAWSON AND

NAVY: RPI MICHEALE PERRY

My step-dad is in the military fighting for my freedom.
He is in Iraq putting his life on the line for my family, my
friends, even people he does not know, and me. He cares
enough to give his life for anyone and everyone. He
may be a million miles away eating popcorn at work, but
he would still be my hero. Before we moved here to
Germany, I could go to work with him. He would make
sure that his friends and other soldiers would not use
profanity or act in an inappropriate ways around me. That
meant a lot to me.

—Kiersten Cade, age 12

ARMY: SFC WILLIAM T. O'BRIAN

My dad gives all of his time into the military. He does Meals on Wheels every Wednesday. Meals on Wheels is a program that gives food to the elderly. My dad is trustworthy because other soldiers' lives are in my dad's hands when he goes to war. He goes to work every day and never misses a day. A hero is not someone who is famous; a hero could be someone just around the corner, or in front of your face, like my dad.

—Christina Cleveland, age 12

AIR FORCE: SMSGT ANTHONY H. CLEVELAND

Christina Akinson, age 11

The military can be very hard sometimes. For example, one night my dad came home and was a little grouchy because the plane he was working on kept breaking. Soon it was time for dinner. But the phone rang, "Ring, Ring, Ring." My dad picked up the phone and said the plane keeps breaking and I can't fix it. My dad ate dinner then went back to work. Now if that happened to me I would be very upset because I wouldn't want to get up to go fix a plane. I really wouldn't want to do that. But he did anyways. He puts the food on the table, pays for piano lessons and for basketball season, clothes, shoes, socks, things for school, bed covers, pillows, jewelry, hair ties, toys and etc. I think if I was ever in the military I would never be able to do as well as my dad. It would take lots of work.

—Whitney Carradine, age 11

AIR FORCE: CMSGT ERNEST R. CARRADINE SR.

My military mom is my hero because she is caring, loving, and my best friend. She has helped me a lot in life whether it's boys or tragedy.

—Ashleigh Harsch, age 13

AIR FORCE: MSGT KRISTINA HAFERMALZ

My mom and dad used to be in the military, but my dad retired so now it is just my mom. Having a military parent is a privilege; I get to travel to foreign countries like England. Another reason I'm glad my mother is in the military is that I get to eat foreign food. I love food.

—Marco Grimsley, age 11

AIR FORCE: SSGT KIMBERLY GRIMSLEY

Xavier Hallmon, age 10

When you go on TDY I feel sad but I also feel proud when I do feel sad I just remember that you will not get hurt and you are doing all you can to help with the war on terrorist. I am very, very, very proud that you are my one and only dad. If I did not have you I would not know what to do. When I need help on my work you do all you can do to help me. When I am down you can make me laugh, when I am upset you can comfort me. I hope that you can help the war and do all that is in your power to help put a stop to it. I hope that you will not retire for a long long time. If you do then I cannot wear my PROUD TO BE A MILITARY BRAT t-shirt any more. But I will love the shirt just the same. I hope that you live to a ripe old age.

—Meaghan T. Hayward, age 11

AIR FORCE: MAJ GARY T. HAYWARD

My dad hangs around with me every day. My dad plays chess with me every day and we are equally matched. We play basketball and it is very challenging but fun to play with him because he makes jokes up as we play. My dad is a Lt. Colonel and he works very hard at his job. He takes his job seriously; he picks something he wants to do and goes for it. Never once did he try to quit or retire as soon as he could, except when my mom was getting annoyed of having to move every two years. He doesn't put me aside and do his work first because he always says "Family before duty." My dad bear hugs me. When he tickles me it seems like everything stops and you're captured in the picture. My family is smiling and we're all having a good time.

—Cody Hartford, age 12

AIR FORCE: LT COL SCOTT HARTFORD

He goes to Iraq for my freedom and his. He saves me from all the bad things in the world. He is the one who disciplines me for all the bad things I do. And so if I am about to do it again I won't because I will remember what he told me when I got into trouble. When I am down he brings me up. He helps me with all the stuff I don't know and then I get the problems right. When I get hurt or sick he makes me feel better. He would be a good grandfather someday because of all the things he did to save me. He is just the best hero I have ever had in my whole life.

—Sydney Clower, age 11

ARMY: SPC MARTIN T. APARICIO

He is in Iraq fighting the war. His job is to give information to soldiers going on a mission. He says it's called S2 Shop. He sometimes goes on a patrol but not usually. He says they have a lot of "Road Side Bombs." When he came home for RR he showed me some pictures of the Road Side Bombs. They were hard to spot on the side of the road. Some were just cans with explosives inside them. He said when he gets in his humvee and is going off his post to the city that he gets a little afraid because he doesn't know what will happen. I am very proud of my dad for what he does.

—Darien J. Larson, age 12

ARMY: SFC CURTIS E. WOOLSEY

She is an inspiration to me. She is strong, getting through the day, even if it's a bad one. She gets me home safe to a warm house with food and water. And she teaches me valuable things on a regular basis.

—Caleb Petersen, age 11

AIR FORCE: TSGT ANN PETERSEN (RET)

He puts his life on the line like Superman. He saves people from hunger and from getting killed by bombs or something else dangerous. He also protects our family not just the people in Iraq. I think that every mom and dad is a hero because they protect their families.

—Jessenia Villalobas, age 11

ARMY: SSG FRANK L. BURKHARD

He is fighting for our nation so we can be safe. He and a friend of his run half the Ledward base even though my dad has a broken back and his friend has plates in his legs. They run to get better and get trained. He is always there for me and my brother and he does so many things for the poor, lost and the ones in pain.

—Jason Kinosh, age 11

ARMY: SSG MICHAEL P. KINOSH

When they disagree they don't do it in front of me. I also like the fact that they don't drink or smoke. My mom and dad try and always make me see the good points in bad situations and that is a big help because without that guidance I would probably be a wreck.

—Mitchell Louis Kimbrough, age 12

ARMY SFC STEVE WARD (RET) AND MRS. DORETHY J. WARD

Hilary Green, age 10

He goes to wars even if he doesn't want to, but he does it anyway if it will help our country. My dad is a very loyal man. He goes to work at 5:00 AM and he doesn't come back till late at night. No matter how late he gets home, he always kisses us goodnight. He is the best soldier and father that anyone could ever have. I just wish he could stay here forever.

—Benjamin Gardner, age 11

ARMY: 2LT ROCKNEE M. GARDNER

He shows respect to everyone. He is in the U.S. Army and he loves it. He's fighting a war right now and he shows courage and bravery. I wish I had as much courage and bravery as he does. Right now he's in Iraq. He has been there almost 5 months now. He is on tanks. For just that he is my hero for working in the heat of the Iraqi desert and on one of those icky tanks. Also for sharing a tent with a few other people. He calls us every day and tells us what it's like and the weather. In September he told us with all of his gear it felt like 200 degrees but it was only 110. That's still really hot. He has to sleep with a lot of bugs and dust because it's so windy there. He told us that they have no air conditioning anywhere. That must get really hot.

—Alexis G. Mitchell-Dugan, age 11

ARMY: SSG GLEN D. BALLANTYNE

He fights to defend our country and I am very proud of him. He goes through sandstorms training the Iraqis, and my mom got upset when we got the news that my dad had shaved his head. It's not easy for him to be gone to a place where catastrophic things happen. I try to hold back my tears when I watch the news and there is suddenly a bombing of cars or any of the kinds of things I worry about all the time. I hate it when he has to be down there in a place where we all fear that something bad is going to happen. This is a very hard mission to accomplish for my dad, which is why I have him for a hero. It makes me proud that he would actually accept the challenge. But then it's hard to be with my mom with no help to take care of me and my brother and sister. My dad would always take care of things around the house even though it annoyed me just doing and redoing my room. He always helped me with my spelling, now it's harder when he's gone because my brother might be the only one to help me. And that is very difficult. Him being gone has its good times and bad. The bad times are when we hear that there is a bombing in Iraq and we are scared that it might be in Camp Liberty, the camp where he stays. Also, on Thanksgiving Day he would always bake the turkey, but this year, when my mom baked it, it was way too hard. But the good times are when he would stop telling me to clean my room. If he ever sees it he would be yelling his head off!

—Orya Lau, age 12

ARMY: SFC FREDERIC W. LAU

The definition of a hero is a man/woman of distinguished courage and ability who is admired for his brave deeds and noble qualities. That in every way is how I see my dad. I admire him for his brave deeds and many noble qualities. My father has multiple characteristics of a hero. My dad is extremely generous. He would give me the shirt off his back. When the light bulb in my room went out, he risked his life to remove it because it broke in the socket. He risked being electrocuted to give me light in my room. He is extremely courageous in his line of work being in the Navy. There are many brave things that my dad does. He would do anything to make sure that I am safe. My

Darien Carson, age 9

dad served in the war in Iraq to make the country safer for us all. He says that is what his job requires of him but I think that is what a hero does. He does not look for recognition of his work, although he definitely deserves it. He has coached my basketball team for the last two years. He also volunteers in the local community. My dad puts others before himself. He works hard in all aspects of his life. I would change the definition of a hero to a man/woman who cares for people, who doesn't worry about getting recognition for what they do. Someone who just does it because it's the right thing to do. That would be my definition of a hero. My dad is the inspiration of that new definition.

—Valacia Titus, age 13

NAVY: SCPO DONOVAN TITUS

My dad: hardworking, athletic, loyal, and funny. He has been in the Marines for 23 years and is currently a colonel working as a lawyer in the Staff Judge Advocate Office. He was inspired by his father who fought in the Marines when he was young. He has fought for his country, which is very brave. He is a lot like me and I look up to him. He is my role model. He is hardworking, loyal, has a good sense of humor and most importantly, he never gives up, and I admire him for that. We spend a lot of time together playing sports and golfing, and even though I beat him we still have a good time in each other's company. Since there are seven kids in my family he has to work hard both at work and at home. He has also had to put up with moving and has been stationed in West Virginia, Hawaii, San Diego, California twice, and Okinawa twice. He has to put up with that and all of my brothers and sisters fighting constantly. He is proud of us and he is a great dad.

Mike Koeneke, age 13

MARINES: COL RICH KOENEKE

My dad is a hero because of his good qualities, leadership, a sense of humor, and a serious attitude when necessary. He has served his country for 20 years, which makes him a veteran. My dad does his job no matter how difficult it is, so he can support his family. Although my dad has never won a battle or done any great achievement in war, he is a great dad and a hero to me.

—Mariah McMinn, age 12

AIR FORCE: MSGT MICHAEL MCMINN

Trey Adkins, age 9

Fighting for his country is what he does best. People respect him because he is responsible, smart, caring, nice, and so much more words cannot describe. His job in the Army is just reviewing everything going on in the world and at war and then telling other people about it. He has never been deployed but he wants to. He is retiring next year, moreover he is going to go to school and try to be a college professor. So that means we are moving (again). He wants to go to Auburn, but I don't because I don't appreciate their college football team, the Auburn Tigers. Although I don't like the team, I am with him 100%. He has told me it is beautiful there and I will love it. (I hope he is right.)

—Joe Townes, age 13

ARMY: COL RICH TOWNES

She was born on September 1, 1970. She was a morning baby who came into this world to do things for other people. She works as a Marine on the Camp Pendleton Base in Oceanside. Right now she is at Cal State San Marcos College for her master's degree so she can become a Major and become the top Marine. She has been in the Marines since she was 18 years old.

—Alexis Richardson, age 13

MARINES: CAPT MARISSA JOHNSON

My dad is confident, sensible, comprehensible, strong, and he is always right about what is good for him and for our family. He is a good, handsome guy and I am happy to have a dad just like him. I think he is the best dad in the world. He is short. He is from Puerto Rico. He spends most of his time fixing his car and he is sometimes a serious man.

—Tanyelis Illueca, age 15

ARMY: SSG JOSE A. MUNOZ

A warm smile and a stern look is how I will always remember my mom. My mother does so much for us and gets so little back. Everyday she keeps on going with steadfast determination. Her qualities range from the kind of kindness that warms people to a silent temper that is absolutely chilling. She works incredibly hard at home and at work. Lucky for me she is not a prude. With all of her stern nature she is fun and loving. She may not have changed the world but she has given a feeling of happiness to all around her.

—Paris Yabuku, age 13

NAVY: CPO GARIZALY YABUKO

John Isbell is a really brave hero. Whenever there is a person drowning in the water, John must jump off the helicopter, swim to the person, and put the person in a little basket. Then the guy in the helicopter pulls it up. Then John goes up after. One day John had a very scary mission. In the middle of the night there was a guy in a boat. There were huge waves and the boat sank. Then my dad jumped off the helicopter and saw to the guy, and put him in the little basket. So my dad saved a person's life. He has accomplished 21 years in the Coast Guard. When he first started it was hard for him because they made him do push-ups, crunches, and swim laps. He also had to go to Antarctica for practice. He did these things almost everyday until he accomplished it and didn't have to practice anymore. He has a big smile when he walks through his work. John Isbell loves saving other people's lives.

—Tyara M. Isbell, age 14

COAST GUARD: PO1 JOHN ISBELL

Every single day my dad dutifully walks out the door to work, but whether working night or day, he, to me, personifies what it really means to be a hero. I plainly remember frequent times where he, in spite of his tired state, played videos or lovingly chastised me if I was behaving badly. Nevertheless, when I am down he encourages me with his predictable hellos to frequent bowling almost all night long. My dad is my rock and my clock all in one. Whether waking me up at four or three in the morning with undisguised enthusiasm to go fishing or just waking me up so I don't sleep the Saturday away. Moreover, I will always remember my dad as a source of light in the most uncomfortable times of my life. He is my foundation of my future self, for no matter how rough life gets he can show a positive side with an amusing joke. Foremost of all are the spirited sacrifices he made while serving in Uzbekistan. I am glad he was there and is here now to spend quality time with my family and I. So many people have broken homes that he is an exceptional living example of what I wish every parent's marriage life to be like. Steady and faithful whether seven in the morning or seven at night he dons his battle dress uniform to go serve our great country.

—Julius Walker, age 13

ARMY: LTC HERMAN H. WALKER JR.

My mom, even though she is not in the military is brave enough to be in the Army! She cooks, cleans, helps us with out homework, washes and folds clothes and assists in activities that we do. She volunteers at my school, teaches Sunday school at church and coaches basketball. She takes care of my brothers and me, even when my dad is away. She is also kind, caring, loving, fair and trustworthy. Sure, she gets upset sometimes, but she does what ever she can do to make our lives better.

—Zach Hunter, age 11

ARMY: MAJ THOMAS HUNTER AND LISA HUNTER

My mom is a great singer! She is a Sergeant First Class singer that sings with the United States Military Academy Band. She sings jazz, gospel, and patriotic songs. When my mom sings people say they're filled with joy because the songs mean so much to her.

—Nyya N. A. Bradley, age 11

ARMY: SFC LAURA R. M. BRADLEY

Ashleigh Mazingo, age 9

The Family Man, that's my dad. My father was a New York City fireman for almost 23 years. My mom says I saved my father's life on September 10, 2001, when I was hospitalized with a leg infection. My dad stayed with me the first night in the hospital. When my mom came to the hospital the next morning (September 11), me and my dad were watching the terrorist attack on television. After the second plane hit the Twin Towers my dad said he had to go there to help. We didn't hear from him till the next day. That day my father lost 6 firefighters from the firehouse where he worked. He took those losses very hard. We, his family, were always by his side during this tragedy. I love my dad very much. I never take my father for granted anymore.

One month after September 11 my father was activated by the United States Coast Guard. He is a very proud member of the Coast Guard for over 20 years. He was happy to serve his country in any way he could. My father is a big believer in respect. He feels if you are respectful to someone they will be respectful to you. Respect starts at home in the family.

My dad is very active in my community. He also participated in the Wounded Warriors Program with the New York City Fire Department. What this group does is to invite wounded veterans to New York City for a weekend. Most of these veterans have lost a leg(s) or arm(s). Last summer I was with my dad when the veterans came to New York and went to the beach for the weekend. I personally found this to be a very rewarding experience. It was so nice seeing those soldiers have a good time. I was surprised how positive these men were about life. They were really an inspiration to me.

My dad is also an inspiration to me! My father does not like to be called a hero. He feels that the people who died on September 11, 2001 and all the soldiers who have died in this current war are the true heroes of today's society. I love my dad; I think he is the best father in the world.

—John Matthew Cullen, age 15

COAST GUARD: MST2 JOHN P. CULLE

My dad serves in the Army. He is a Colonel and has his own building! When he comes home late we immediately have dinner. I wait until 8:00 PM to ask him to check my homework. We spend about an hour doing homework because my dad wants me to get good grades. Sometimes I get mad because I have to do the questions over but in the end I know it will help me. When he finds a problem that's incorrect he doesn't just tell me the right answer because he wants me to solve it myself. When I ask him why, he says it's for practice. My dad almost never cooks and cleans, but when he does I can tell my mom thinks he's a helpful hero because he is helping her. Sometimes he does the dishes and the laundry. He puts the dishes in the dishwasher and that is a big help to my mom. I bet my mom enjoys it when he carries the laundry up the stairs.

—Meghan Kenyon, age 10

ARMY: COL ROBERT KENYON

He is so brave with or without weapons. Most people think that a hero has to have super powers or super strength. That is not true. Having courage to stand up for what you believe in does. Just a couple of years ago he was deployed to Afghanistan and was under attack when he was sleeping at 3:30 in the morning. He did not have any super powers, the only thing he had was his brain and his M16. (A type of gun.) He went outside and started giving his soldiers instructions on what to do. One of the soldiers didn't listen to what my dad said, and that could have cost everyone their lives. The soldier went on top of a Jeep to grab his gun; my dad saw a terrorist about to shoot him and ran to pull the soldier down. All of my dad's unit had to retreat because most of them were dead. My dad has never been wounded while training for battle, and I don't ever want him to start. Thanks to my father I am alive and healthy in this world. My daddy is my hero because he takes the time to do things; he doesn't just do them to get it over with. He does it with care and to do it right and completely.

—June M. Tug, age 13

ARMY: SFC JOHN TUG

My mom is an attorney for the Air Force. She has been a prosecutor, a defense attorney, and she gives legal advice to commanders. All of these jobs are important. She goes through many struggles on TDY, but she never gives up. One of the struggles she goes through is loss of sleep. Between travel and court preparation my mom can get pretty tired.

—Charli Gruen, age 12

AIR FORCE: CAPT PATRICIA GRUEN

How can I explain my dad? I know my dad is a hero because he has a heart as wide and open as the sea. I guess that's why they say from sea to shining sea. He is a colonel in the United States Army. He has fought in many places like Afghanistan, Saudi Arabia, and Israel for months at a time. Every time he was gone I would pray for him every night. Even though he was in Saudi Arabia for four months he still thought about me and my siblings. He was there over Christmas which was hard on the family. He recorded himself on a tape, singing, playing the guitar and talking to us. I know it sounds simple, but when you are in a situation like that and someone takes time to do that for you, it is like the touch of an angel.

—Clare Virginia Zupan, age 13

ARMY: COL DANIEL S. ZUPAN

My father is my hero for many reasons. Not only does he provide my family with some of the things we have now (i.e. furniture, electronics, etc.) but he works hard to get them. I also like that he is in the military because he is someone that I want to be when I get old enough. I plan to graduate from the Naval Academy, join the Navy and work myself up to become a captain or some other important rank like himself. He is someone I can look up to when I need help. I often ask him for help with my Social Studies and Science homework and every time he has helped me do it, I got a good grade on whatever the homework was. He is also good, parental wise. He is probably just like any parent, he's nice when I do things when I'm told and constantly on my case when I slack off on my homework or household chores. But if I do things when I am told and accomplish them he rewards me with either a raised allowance or trust so that I have more freedom traveling on and off base. He is truthful and can be counted on. Like, if he broke a lamp, or if he got into a bag of chips, he will definitely fess up and say that he did it. And if I ask for a ride to school at 6:45 AM he will keep his promise and drive me to school at 6:45 AM. So, overall, my dad would have to be my one and only hero.

—Kevin Holz, age 12

NAVY: CMDCM WILLIAM C. HOLZ

My dad is so supportive; he is there whenever I need him. He is there whenever they are in need. He always shows leadership traits, it takes a lot to put him down. He is tough, thrives when needed, pushes himself to his limits and he's a definite fighter. He is the provider for my family and the reason why I breathe today. When I was little I remember he would always tell me of his life in the Army. I always loved hearing it. I looked up to him then and I still do now. He calls himself Superman. Well, he isn't the Superman that we all know today. But he surely is the Superman in my family. My dad is very brave and tough. He doesn't like pain; if he's in pain he tries his best not to show it. When he is about to cry he holds back every tear until there's no more to hold back. To others he may just be a typical dad and not so great, but nobody's perfect. He'll always be great to me and my family no matter what happens. I love him and always will.

—Samantha Carnay, age 13

NAVY: PO2 DENNIS CAPIENDO

She helps me when I am hurt really bad. She makes the best cheese sandwiches. When she comes home she tickles me and plays with me. She takes me to Chili's if she has time.

—Christian Ritter, age 7

ARMY: CPT ALFREDA B. RITTER

If it weren't for both of them I would not be here today. Sometimes I might be rude, or give them a smelly attitude, but I will always love them. I hope and wish every day that they will never ever leave me. I am sure if you were me you would choose them too, they are great parents.

—Joel Mercado, age 13

NAVY: LT ROBERT MERCADO (CHAPLAIN)

My hero is a career air force officer. She is an Air Force Academy graduate, a high school All-American basketball player and a college basketball star. My mom has made from Lieutenant to Colonel in minimum time and has been a distinguished graduate in all of her schools. She has worked hard to get where she is, but most of all she loves us very much. Heroes are special. They have a special place in life because of their impact on others. My hero is my mom.

—Brianna Gladney, age 11

AIR FORCE: COL AMANDA W. GLADNEY

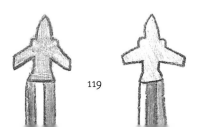

If my Dad was not in the military my life would be so much different and maybe yours too. My father is a Chief and has been in the Military for about 20 years. He and many have worked hard to help others and to gain a high rank. My dad's job is working on computers. He can fix any computer and even build one. Cool, huh! I'm very proud of my dad. He is able to get on a ship and not be afraid of what's in the water or if something goes wrong. I can't do that because I have a fear of water, but my dad is an example of someone who can do anything even if they are scared to do it. I want to be like that when I grow up. From being in the military my dad is not lazy like I am (sometimes, not all the time am I lazy). He used to get up every morning about six to go run for his P.T. It takes guts to do that, because your body can be sore from working out every day, but he did it. When I leave to go to college I'll have some of the traits he gave me. I hope the lazy ones go away so I won't be late for my classes!

Jasmin Conyers, age 14

NAVY: CPO RICHARD CONYERS

He went to Afghanistan and sacrificed his life for his country and the people in it. My dad was killed in Afghanistan on November 27th. Just because he went to war and died is not the only reason he is my hero. He was always there for me in life and death. He always knew what was right and kept me on task. He helped me with my homework and my school. When I found out that he had died I was devastated but I knew he was in a better place and that he will always look over me. I know that he will always be happy because he was so funny. My dad isn't the only hero I have. My mom was always there for me. Even though we have fights we still love each other and the bond is unique and special. When my dad died she went through so much grief but she was still there for us and we were there for her. Anyone who can go through that and can come out on top of things is my hero.

Thomas Matthew McMahon, age 13

ARMY: COL JEANETTE MCMAHON AND
LTC MICHAEL J. MCMAHON (KIA NOV. 27, 2004)

Abigael Bylow, age 6

My dad is my hero because he helps save the world.

—Chantal Riep, age 12

ARMY: SPC RICHARD T. JOHNSON

He makes his soldiers believe in themselves. He's training tomorrow's Army and in my opinion he's doing a pretty good job.

—Savannah Brock, age 11

ARMY: CSM FREDDIE BROCK

Every day he goes off to work and has the chance of being hurt, but he goes to work all the same. He helps people all the time and comes home and still has the energy to be a great father. He's funny and acts weird sometimes but that is one of the reasons I like him so much. He always acts like life isn't full of ups and downs but just ups. He loves his job and goes all over the world, even if the place is too damp or too hot. On top of it all, he's always home on time. This makes my mom very happy.

—Molly Mueller, age 11

AIR FORCE: SMSGT ROBERT MUELLER

My dad is in school to get a higher rank, to start with. He works awfully hard in school. He goes every Monday and Wednesday. He doesn't get home until really late. I mean really late. One time he didn't get home until 1:00 in the morning. Talk about cranky! My dad is always helping others at the same time. One time he babysat a little girl for two hours. It was long! Finally he has raised five girls. I bet it's hard work because we all need food, clothes, supplies and other needs. I also bet it's fun. In the morning when my dad flies off to work, there are five kisses from us five girls. I feel special for a dad like him. He's the best, well, I mean next to my mom.

—Morgan Bogue, age 11

AIR FORCE: MAJ BRIAN BOGUE

Before he deployed he talked to my brother and I, and he told us not to be afraid. He said when it is dark to always pray for his safe return. Even though he is not here his humor always fills my house and though we cannot see him, his love and hope are with us. Whenever I make a mistake he is right there to tell me not to worry. Whenever I am down, angry and scared he is there to calm me down. I would not give up my dad for anything. Not even a mountain of gold.

—Andrea Vidargas, age 12

ARMY: SSG LUIS R. VIDARGAS

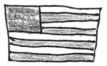

Contributors

Aspen Abram

Trey Adkins

Christina Akinson

Cody Anderson-Parks

Jourdan Barrows

Samantha A. Beyers

Kathryn Bistodeau

Hadley Boberg

Morgan Bogue

Nyya N. A. Bradley

Sean Brannon

Savannah Brock

Nyesha Brownlee

Hunter Burbank

Abigael Bylow

Kiersten Cade

Sean Callahan

Samantha Carnay

Whitney Carradine

Darien Carson

Analysa Cassanova-Smith

Christina Cleveland

Sydney Clower

Jasmin Conyers

Shae Corey

John Matthew Cullen

Katie Deal

Joseph R. Diaz

Kylie Dillinger

Kate Donnellan

Psalms Doucettperry

Meghan Duffey

Hannah Dunks

Kaleb Dunks

Jerrel Elder

Mark Estrada

Morgan Flick

Abagail Frantzen

Benjamin Gardner

Laura Isabel Gilchrist

Mercedes Gillon-Gantt

Blaise Giove

Brianna Gladney

Hilary Green

Johnathon Greenhoe

Marco Grimsley

Charli Gruen

Xavier Hallmon

Brandon Jordan Hansen

Ashleigh Harsch

Cody Hartford

John Harvey

Meaghan T. Hayward

Ally Heitink

Destanie Heslar

Kevin Holz

Kelsey Hover

Zach Hunter

Reed Hurdertmark

Tanyelis Illueca

Tyara M. Isbell

Kimberly Kavinsky

Meghan Kenyon

Charles Kim

Mitchell Louis Kimbrough

Veronica King

Jason Kinosh

Matthew Klempp

Mike Koeneke

Dasia Lang

Darien J. Larson

Orya Lau

Brittany Learn

Roland Lester

Samuel Niall Lindsey

Shaniquah Lipki

Christopher Lipscomb

Ladasia Logan

Emma Mallets

Ashleigh Mazingo

Jake McCrea

Veronica McLeod

Thomas Matthew McMahon

Mariah McMinn

Joel Mercado

Alexis G. Mitchell-Dugan

Emilly Mueller

Molly Mueller

Avery Nelson

Butler Nicklus

Courtney Ortega

Robert Osborn

Thomas Overtree

Jennifer Patino

Taylor Paul

Sarah Pearson

Zachari Perri

Markeith Perry

William Peters

Caleb Petersen

Shepard Todd Petit

Cotey Pierce

Jessie Reeves

Alicia Reynolds

Emily Elisabeth Rhea

Alexis Richardson

Chantal Riep

Christian Ritter

John Robert

Esperanza Rosales

Colin Ryan

Brandon Shelton

Raymond Joseph Shew

Cheyenne Slaton

Astrid Sletten

Aidan Sloan

Zechariah Snel

Jacob Snow

Gabrielle Tan

John Ward Tatum III

Megan Thomas

Cathryn Thompson

Valacia Titus

Sharim E. Torres

Joe Townes

Nathaniel Tripp

June M. Tug

Zachery Tyra

Ellie Varicak

Andrea Vidargas

Jessenia Villalobas

Julius Walker

Devin Ward

Kirstyn Wesala

Tessa Wilcox

Jazzmine Willis

Susi Wills

Ariel Wilson

Kanyon Wilson

Robert Anthony Windom Jr.

Paris Yabuku

Clare Virginia Zupan

John Robert, age 11